The Waters of Appanoose County

by Garry L Cox

Eileen

Thank you for your recent
reminder that back the
tempestuous days of our
youth I shared my dream
of becoming a published
author. Who knew it would
take so long :)

Love, Garry

Published in the United States by Global Athlete Media Network.

St. Louis, MO

ISBN-10: 0-9981339-1-4

ISBN-13: 978-0-9981339-1-1

Table of Contents

About the Title:

In the spirit of introducing myself, I'd like to share the fact that in my seventy plus trips around the sun I have received many kudos for my writing skills. A friend of mine told me back in high school that anybody who could produce cognitive text in a variety of social and professional settings would do well in life. Ok, maybe he didn't say it so succinctly, it was high school. But that was his gist. And he was right. I have three careers and a Masters Degree under my belt to prove it. But what I'm also sharing is my response to the kind words that have come my way. The conversation has varied only slightly over the years. Here's a taste.

Kind Soul: I really like the way you write. You're so easy to follow, and I always get where you're coming from.

Garry: Thank you for the kind words. But you know, I can't take much credit for it. I was born and raised in Iowa. Appanoose County to be exact.

Kind Soul: What has Iowa got to do with it?

Garry: Have you ever heard of the Iowa Tests of Educational Development?

Kind Soul: Yeah, I think I may have taken that test back in the day.

Garry: Well, they don't call it the I O W A test for nothing.

(1) University of Iowa, baby. Came out in 1942. Year I was born.

Kind Soul: *(looking dubious)* Not sure I see the connection.

Garry: Try harder. Here's another clue. University of Iowa Writer's Workshop. Familiar with that?

Kind Soul: *(beginning to look less kind)* I might have heard of it.

Garry: *(Warming to his subject)* Well, let me just tell you. It is no accident that for seven decades the University of Iowa Writers Workshop produced over half the renowned writers in the history of writing. (2)

Kind Soul: That's pretty impressive. So that's where you went to school?

Garry: No, I went to Missouri State Teacher's College (*Truman University now*).

Kind Soul: *(losing it)* So what the hell does Iowa have to do with your writing?

Garry: I don't know, really. I think it might just be something in the water. I did tell you I was from Appanoose County didn't I?

I have told variations of this story many times, mainly so whoever I'm talking to won't think I take myself too seriously. But in my high school graduating class of roughly 150 kids, I was maybe the third best writer. In My CLASS.

Why poetry and Why now?

Why poetry?

Reason 1: It was my computer's fault.

A catastrophic computer glitch wiped out major portions of three unfinished novels and two finished plays. I wouldn't have most of the poems in this book if a caring soul hadn't backed them up for me along the way.

Reason 2: It was my mother's fault.

I just have this childhood memory of a time when I would wake up with some nebulous imagery that had to be shared at all costs. Kind of a cross between an epiphany and an 'aha' moment. Or maybe a brainstorm. My mother, Zoe, was the target of my early morning outbursts. And she seemed to give them almost as much importance as I did. But as centuries passed (kid years are way shorter than dog years) my mother started calling these outbursts 'poems'. Whatever! She seemed to delight in them. So I delighted too. But more eons pass, I've discovered the great outdoors, and I simply don't have time for mom constantly nagging me for some silly 'poems' I don't even have anymore.

Reason 3: Love notes

From 1997 to 2008 when I retired from Rio Salado College, I composed a poem for my wife Bernice every day before I left for work. I wrote on a 2' by 3' white board that I had filched from my Learning Center. Little ditties I usually made up in the shower. Love notes that depicted stuff from our daily lives. It was fun for me, and Bernice loved to start her day with coffee and a poem. Occasionally she would chide me, "I didn't get my poem this morning." She didn't have to chide me often.

Bernice's daughter Ellen would also check the white board whenever she visited us. She once suggested to her mother that instead of simply erasing the board as was her habit, she should record and try to publish the poems since I'd written way more than enough for a book. Her response was typical Bernice. "They're my poems. I don't need to share them with the world."

Why Now?

Well, 'Now' is the new buzz word for sure. But it's also one of those Yin Yang things. On the one hand 'Now' is the absolute right-this-nano-second Present. On the other hand, 'Now' started the moment I was born and won't be 'Then' till the moment I pass over. So either I started writing poetry an instant before Word went into auto-save, or I had a rhyme in mind when the doctor smacked me on the bottom. Take your pick.

Early Influences

Just in case you are under 60, the mean age of most of my friends, I apologize for not having the wherewithal to provide the social media bells and whistles you are no doubt accustomed to. For example, as I write this a Sam Cook tune is wafting through 'the corners of my mind". I think you might like this tune as much as your parents and grandparents did, but I can only provide the lyrics. YouTube Sam up and enjoy the poetry of my youth.

Don't know much about history

Don't know much biology

Don't know much about a science book,

Don't know much about the French I took

But I do know that I love you,

And I know that if you love me, too,

What a wonderful world this would be

Now, I don't claim to be an "A" student

But I'm trying to be

For maybe by being an "A" student baby

I can win your love for me

So this is me, still trying to be an "A" student, baby. Trying to share my reflections on life, love and the Yin and Yang of our existence on this planet. Which includes my search for a sustaining faith. My spiritual evolution is still very much a work in progress.

The biggest Yin Yang for me has always been that of Truth on the one hand and Perception on the other. *(Am I starting to sound like Tevye in Fiddler on the Roof?)* Do they oppose each other, or do they work together on some harmonious plane? Or am I oversimplifying? What about Reality?

My take on Reality is that it's a lot like the net in a tennis match. It's only necessary if you're keeping score. I try not to keep score.

The following poem was a starting point for me. I wrote it long before I grew into it.

Without Faith There is No Peace

Without faith there is no peace

I choose faith

Lead me Lord to stronger faith

Without peace there is no joy

I choose peace

Guide me Lord to deeper peace

Without joy life is empty

I choose joy

Fill me Lord with your eternal joy

Spirit

The Tale of Ralphie and the Black Cat

So the story goes, a Cleric, an Atheist and an Agnostic are taking turns stepping into a room of total darkness and unknown depth. Their task, find the black cat that may or may not be roaming somewhere in the void. The Cleric goes first and after a time returns and proclaims, "I found the rascal. I searched long and hard and nearly gave up, but I got my hands on his furry body and stroked his head before he escaped me. He's in there alright."

The Atheist went next and came back with a different report, "I found exactly what I expected to find. Nothing. No cat and no cat's meow."

The last to report was the Agnostic. "You know, I'm not sure if I found him or not. There were times when I thought I did. Might of heard him. Even smelled him. Then I thought I was probably just smelling my own cat, Ralphie, on my clothes and I gave up the search."

My greatest hope is that you see in these poems, a man exploring the possibility of true faith. My greatest fear is that you see in them a man who claims he has found it.

Of all the concepts of truth I'm aware of, irony is my favorite. Of course the ultimate irony is a just and loving God of an unjust and hateful world. But it's the smaller ironies of human existence that most capture my imagination. For example, the following quote from W.

Somerset Maugham, an avowed atheist, is the sweetest example of God's love I ever heard.

"And isn't it wonderful that with those simple objects, with his painter's exquisite sensibility, moved by the charity in his heart, that funny, dear old man should have made something so beautiful that it breaks you? It was as though, unconsciously perhaps, hardly knowing what he was doing, he wanted to show you that if you only have enough love, if you only have enough sympathy, out of pain and distress and unkindness, out of all the evil of the world, you can create beauty."

- W. Somerset Maugham, Christmas Holiday

When it comes to my own faith, I am merely a seeker. Sort of a 'now you see it, now you don't' sort of fellow. But my stumbling path is strewn with gems that say to me, "Yes, you can run with this for a while."

"Holy Faith gives us an unshakable confidence in the inherent goodness of life and of the universe."

(enneathought@enneagraminstitute.com)

Upon a Velvet Invitation

Upon a velvet invitation

to go deeper into the silence

of a silent prayer in church

I became a seasoned sprinter,

exploding with a fury

into to the unforgiving matrix

of distance over time.

I became a pusher for a bobsleigh,

churning madly for speed enough

to jump into the missile

and hurl me down the icy slope

I became the lost one

who died upon the curve

and floated in the black

feeling terror in my error

I became the found one

with solid chair beneath me

tooling with a quiet calmness

into the void of Peace

Tennis Anyone?

Here I sit dated and boiler-plated

Arrogant in the illusion of my naked body

Doubtful of all human histories

Yet mindful of their vaults and cemeteries

Knowing I've been here before

but how or what or who

Believing I'll never die

yet fearing the requisite transformation

I hold as certain that Heaven will have me

which begs the question, will I have heaven?

Do I get to choose the terms as was the case with faith?

In darkened dreams I've glimpsed the great Oneness

but from the outside looking in

with no opinion one way or another

Yet here I admit to a leap of faith

and a promise for the other side

Believing I reside inside my soul

and not the other way around

surely my soul has sheltered other me's

and I would like to meet one

Begging its pardon and by its leave

this is what I long to say, ward to ward

If you are me and I am you-

no matter who came first

or who is still to come-

What in heaven is our take

on this eternal holding pattern,

with its constant coming from and going to?

Blessings Flying at Me from All Directions

Blessings flying at me from all directions

Pouring over me

As though I were a stone in a happy stream

Gratitude's just grazing

On my synaptic fields

Like sunflowers along a river bank

When I sit in your presence now

Things are different

Gone are the days

When I called you, tongue in cheek

The Great Spirit of All Good In the Universe

For I have come to know you as Father

And the one true source of peace

I am not only a child of God

But also a good son who honors his Father

By sitting still in his presence

Open to his counsel

If Tomorrow Tames Today

If tomorrow tames today

As I may already have implied

lately my days are filled with fuzziness

a mist like confusion

a nagging discontent

I can't quite put my finger on

Unlike so many other times

after a wondrous night of holy intimacy

when I would wake with peace and gratitude

and find myself floating, flying,

singing through my day

I've been plodding, pacing, spacing

tip-towing around my ego messaging

watching worse case scenarios

turn conveniently to hope

deluding and concluding and back again

Yet yesterday's meditations, mushy and opaque

today became transformed

into beacons of transparency

harkening back to simple choices

faith, love, joy, and hope

Fears have faded but not fled

Want driven questions stay the course

but I came calmly close

to peace on one condition:

Face your fears and give them up to God

Credit to the clouds I say

which disallowed the sun to sting my eyeballs

reminding me that there is no glare

emanating from God's light

There is simply love if one uncoats the lens

If tomorrow tames today

and I am then who I would be now,

a child of God quickening to the light,

framed in freedom clearly gained,

while stillness stays my mind,

my true intentions will have the final say

Good Morning Lord

Good morning Lord

your sunrise keeping promise to the moon

Good morning hope

Still here, though oft I bid you leave

Good morning heart

My, you're feeling light today

Good morning soul

So eager for your prayer

Good morning love

As bright and perfect as the day

My Mind Defeats Me

My mind defeats me
with its incessant fixing

and my ego holds its structure

with diamond nano-threads

while my soul, with deference to neither

holds sovereign over both

What Is the Soul If Not for Longing

What is the soul if not for longing

For seeking the great oneness

in ever greater measure?

And what is the body if not for holding

For imagining the potential

of the unnecessary and the forgotten?

And what are dreams if not for unfolding

For facing the archetypes of our earthly existence

as they play out our hopes and fears?

And what is truth if not for telling

For speaking from our highest selves

to whom we are most accountable?

The Universe of Me

Sitting upright in my bed

I made this journey in my head

As I was trying hard to be so still

and get beyond my stubborn will

and become the one who watches all

I could not escape the noisy thrall

I pitched it skyward but it remained a shroud

and I was stuck with head in cloud

But then I chanced to look below

and saw not houses row on row

but a tiny blob of wetness I took to be a sea

and through the Spirit's Will it beckoned me

'Let go, let go' it seemed to say

'Let go your trying hard, let go the fractured fray

Let go your fear of falling

Your universe is calling

I am but a molecule a million miles away

You will cease to yearn for stars

when you sense how vast you are'

And so I fell and fell and fell

and in falling felt so free

I was one with God in the universe of me

I'm All Right with That Lord

I had a thought this morning Lord

in the midst of meditation,

revelation, elevation-

That you love everything,

the all in your creation

equally, without distinction

That you love the fly

biting at my ankles

every bit as much as you love me

I'm alright with that Lord

Thanks to you I see that love is love

and all there really is

I see that love is something I can choose

to accept and freely give

to all beings in my given realm

including this danged ankle biting fly

My Version of the 23 Psalm

Oh Great Spirit of all good in the universe,

be you my Sheppard and free me from want

Lead me to green pastures beyond my busy golf course

Help me be still beside the stillness of your presence

Reveal to me the path to your unconditional love

Yea, though I walk through the imaginings of my own demise

Let me know that all changes obey your will and abide in your love

Replace all thoughts of rod and staff with your enfolding arms

May the table I share with my enemies be set with gratitude and understanding

Hold my head in your hands as you fill my ever expanding heart with love

May goodness and mercy arise from me even as they do from you

Bless my intention to build, maintain and cherish

a home for our never-ending communion

Sitting in the Spirit's Presence

Sitting in the Spirit's Presence

I am still but hardly stationary

calm but nowhere near collected

seeking but unsought

still hung up on relative position

the Spirit's light above

the light in me below

my ego with its army

blathering in between

me caught up in conundrum

How does light from up above

dive deftly through the dense debris

without picking up impurities?

Slowly came a shift,

the quintessential paradigm

If I am image of the Spirit

we should travel much the same

So I rose up and had a looking down at me

sitting yet in Spirit's light

a witness to my open heart

The armies of confusion

no longer hold their lines

surrender their connections

and wait to be dispersed

like solitary soldiers

harmless and unarmed

Spirit, I Do Not Come to You Today

Spirit, I do not come to you today
the way I have so many times of late
Grateful for my blessings
Seeking to be still
Basking in your presence
Guided by your light
Nurturing my faith

Our space is now so crowded, clouded by my mind
Telling me that God can wait
There is a wound that needs attending
There is blame to cast
There is fear that needs be spread
An attitude must be assumed
A hurt must be returned

Yet there is a question I would ask, Lord
That exists above my busy mind
How can my love for my companion
Manifest itself in such a manner
That strengthens both of us
To follow our separate paths
Yet know we do not go alone

As We Keep Moving, Growing

As we keep moving, growing

going with the changes

in our personal and spiritual lives

I'm reminded of the requirements

Of singing out a song

From the heart, yes

From ones truest self, yes

But there is one abiding certainty in music

It is a journey through time

And every note and syncopation

Exists only to lead one to the next

To truly live, a song must be a leap in faith

That every sour note or out of rhythm phrase
must be forgiven to be open to the story

that flows through the beginning and the end

And then exists forever

Family

Prologue

My birth family was small. Dad, mom, two brothers. It got smaller when I was very young. My brothers ran off to the military and my dad died when I was seven. Growing up with just me and mom, I was equal parts jealous and resentful of family relationships. I was jealous because my friends with larger families never had to play alone as I often did. And I was resentful because I thought the family' exerted a tyrannical influence over its members. Basically, that just meant that it often restricted my access to my friends.

So of course I vowed to remain single for the rest of my life-to play whatever fields opened up to me. Mostly wine, women and song I'm thinking. Fortunately, my field-playing was modest although I did come of age in the Sixties and you know what that means. I am blessed to have ties with three families directly, along with their extended families. I wish I could write a poem about every single member of every single family.

Her Grandson Getting Married

Her grandson getting married

would have made your Grammy happy

To see you decked in full-blown celebration

of a life already full of promise and achievements

would have made your Grammy proud

To be with you and family on this day of days,

surrounded by the best of friends

would have sweetly burst her heart

So look for her between the notes of your wedding
song

smiling shyly amongst the handshakes and the
embraces

And know she's there for you as only she could be

As for the lovely bride, Teresa

Grammy long ago adopted

loved and cherished you

as a dear and proper soul mate

whose independent spirit

has so enhanced your partnership-

I bid you look for my Bernice as well

And so my running buddy, G-man

And Salsa Saucy sister, Lady-T

Being older than I am wise

I have scant advice to give

Cause I see you got it goin' on

So bring it till they 'hallah'

And take it to the house

And hear this mighty shout-out

from Grammy's little mouse!

With all my heart and all my blessings

GG

Ode to Brownie

Dear Brownie

Just a line to let you know

you were the best dog ever lived

because you were my dog

because you were my friend

I thought you might want to know

that you were my last dog, too

My very last

Mom said God took you

Dad said poor judgment did you in

You did love chasing cars, you know

So I figured if God took you

Only God could give me another dog

and he never did

Some might say you had a hard scrabble life

never allowed in the house unless it was freezing
outside

never had a house of your own

Dad built you a lean-to and said it had to do

You never got to hang around the dinner table

and beg for scraps like some dogs were allowed to do

Mom said back on the farm

animals had to earn their keep

and pets should fend for themselves

So I always saved you some supper

and fed you on the porch

Dad was always saying I should tie you up

at night or whenever we would leave

Neighbors said I should have you on a leash

The only time I ever saw you mad

was when I tied a rope around your neck

and tried to pull you for a walk

I gave that up soon enough

Anyway who wants a dog

that won't just follow you around

because it wants to

We did buy you a nifty leather collar though

with Brownie stenciled on a little brass plate

That was just in case you got lost

a finder could read your name

and figure you must be Garry's Brownie

You were never much for showing off

Words like 'fetch' and 'sit' and 'roll over'

 just weren't in your vocabulary

But whenever I would talk to you

your eyes would focus on my face

and you would listen like you understood

Then there was the fun we had

Remember when I tried to push you in the tire swing

And you were too scared to jump out

When the swing died down you just hung there

like a trussed up ring of sausage

You were better in the wagon though

Standing like a general watching his troops go by

Remember Halloween

The time I took you to an outdoor party

And us kids all bobbed for apples

I guess you felt like one of us

But it did create a ruckus

when you slipped between me and a pal of mine

and glommed onto an apple for yourself

trapping it against the side of the tub

like you'd been doing it all you life

Then taking off like a thief

leaving me to bare your scolding

But best of all I think for both of us

were the hours we spent exploring

the mystery of our secret woods

Me searching for Indians and lost gold

and maidens in distress

And you the mighty hunter

chasing anything that moved

including fish floating near the surface of the pond

I believe to this day you could have caught one

if you'd had more stealth than splash

Some say you were a mongrel dog

no lineage to your name

but I say you come from a long line of Brownies

I've seen you through the years, white with big brown splotches

Or the other way around

Hanging with a boy or girl

Companion dogs of the highest order

And you were my Brownie

I was proud to be your kid

I'll remember you forever

Will you remember me?

Squirrels in the Attic

I awoke this morning to a scurrying of something overhead

Squirrels in the attic?

You haven't had an attic in 60 years

Neighbors above me?

Off on a trip, last I heard

Oh yes, oh yes

It's my grandchildren, Scarlett and Theo

Of course, two little sunflowers surging for the sun

Escaping from the stillness of the family bed

Knowing mom is sure to follow

Theo hell bent to explore everything behind every door

Happy to be distracted by a juicy drawer

Scattering objects in his wake

Scarlett dedicated to an early start on her allotted TV time

Vigilant to the assemblage of her appointed audience

Mom and Dad and me

Oh yes, oh yes

Once more it comes, my blessed dilemma

Should I celebrate my waking

by reveling in the sounds of family rising

Smiling in my bed, in my heart

Or should I race to join the fray

knowing mom and coffee are sure to follow

How coldly comes the answer

They've gone back to Kansas City

It was the scurry of your brain, then

Peeling back the numbness of your heart

so it could assimilate your loss

and begin anew to search the question

Will I be alright, being once again alone

Oh yes, oh yes

My faith would have it so

Oh yes, oh yes

But oh....

Ode to Amy

There is something about a river

that provides my greatest clue to you

Wide when the earth allows

seeping out through rocks and loam and sand

common to the lowlands, the flatlands,

the great basins sprouting grains

spreading from the water's edge

across the storied plains

Narrow when created new

or driven deep by granite walls

far below the influence of the sun

Not content to rage along the surface

nor to counterfeit a deadly calm

She would have us know of her geology

the sources of her currents and her undertows

She would have us know her passion

for living full her moments of intention

Have us know her gratitude

for each renewing raindrop

that joins her in her play

Ever seeking promise

in something greater than herself

Ever seeking holy sanction

to shed her mighty singularity

Until she bursts at last

upon the oneness of the ocean

receiving unconditional welcome

knowing wholeness without struggle

peaceful in the wisdom of God's way

To the Daughter We Named Brett

Though you were aptly named

according to your mom and me

It was from a white man's book

which has troubled me of late

We should have had the Indians name you

for they have vision in these things

This attestment comes from me:

From the day you were born

you've been solid in your place

sturdy in your bones

steadfast in your ways

Now let the Indians say through me

these are names you've grown to be

One who gives honor to her heritage?

One who loves her family

One who is constant in her loyalties

One who stands for her convictions

One who fights for fairness

One who has her shit together

One who fears no heights

One who conquers water

One who will not be slighted

One who does not accept dichotomy

One who minces not her words

One who takes pride in her work

One who holds accountable

One who hides her vulnerability

One who falls a lot

One who sings with power

One who holds a godly spirit in her heart

One whose eyes enfold the universe

I do believe these names ring true

But they are not the sum of you

You are more than we can see

The more you are the more you'll be

Brett unfolding in her light

her soul ascending unnamed heights

Ain't We a Pair

Prologue

What I'm sharing here is my personal Noah's Ark. The couples and odd couplings that brought joy or something like it into my life for no reason other than they wanted to.

I Know God Made Hummingbirds to Fly

I know God made hummingbirds to fly

But I don't know why

this particular humming bird

flitted in about head high

and looked me right in the eye

And I don't know why

but thought I should try

to share his impertinence with you

A Solitary Hummingbird from Nowhere

A Solitary hummingbird from nowhere

Punched a hole in the theory of an endless sky

and stopped my wandering mind dead in its tracks

"Behold my singularity," said she

Then camouflaged herself in speed

before my smile could morph into hello

Leaving me with naught to do

But frame her thus and forward her to you

A Sprightly Kitten Called Life

A sprightly kitten called Life

spied the golden ball of yarn called We

batted and teased and unloosed strands

in a flurry of unraveling

and then romped off

Leaving us to wonder

when it would return

to finish what it started

Oh What a Night It Was

Oh what a night it was

Affirming, as it did, the connections of the day

intentions newly found and freely shared

A night of odd-ball appetites

Me in need to cap our unrestrained frivolity

You just happy to eat a catsup packet

Carry-outs

In & Outs

Laughing bouts

Often hokey

Like karaoke

Who needs Keats

And who needs Shelly

When we can dance

Belly to belly

Oh the looks we gave

Some with names and some without

Some in need of acting out

Some amusing

Some we hate

Some confusing

Some a struggle to relate

The "bug" look has me like an insect bound

by your cool discerning eye

Should I be dismissed to fly

Or should I be crushed upon the ground

My "are you sure about that look"

Peering over glasses with knitted brow

Framed of late with whiskers white

What to call it gave you pause

Until you tagged it "the Santa Clause"

You with your "Yeah, like that could ever happen"
look

Or your "That's nice. Go ahead and think that, if it
makes you happy" look

Me with my pouty victim look

Or my "Oh jeez. Not that shit again" look

With its variation "I don't believe you're going there"
look

The look you gave me standing at the door

as we said goodnight and little more

Was made with twinkling eye

causing me to deeply sigh

and drink in the kindness of your face

as a promise in your smile kept pace

When our farewells had all been said

That look accompanied me to bed

Oh what a night it was

Who needs Keats

And who needs Shelly

When we can dance

Belly to belly

One and Done: My Sporting Side

Not To Taut Sadness

Not to tout sadness

But except for March Madness

Nothing under the sun

Is ever one-and-done

No Matter How Fast We Run

No matter how fast we run
How far we throw
or how high we fly
the earth will claim our mortal forms
and we will wait
like ordinary men and women
for our spiritual transformation
But until that day
We are free to set the pace
raise the bar
and claim the glory that is ours
because we are athletes

garrycox.com Blog Living a Dream

Ode to Chad

This was our Olympics

Dave's and Chad's and mine
and Steve's and on and on
Through ALTIS and beyond
Borders and boundaries and barriers
fiercely guarding the un-promised land
And yet we share this noble bond
We all bore witness to the deluge of dreams
that rallied to a single cry
'Let me see how great I can be'

*Cast of characters: Dave Doerrer, Chad Stoermer,
Steve Lewis, ALTIS World.com & garrycox.com*

Love on the Hardwood

March Madness

Catapults us off the shelf

No slice of life but life itself

Baptism in fire

Extinguishing ire

Engendering glee

Killing ennui

Rekindling love for all the above

Ignore the scoops

Because it's hoops

Hopes will narrow

With the possession arrow

We pick our pets

And hedge our bets

And hear all the racquet

About all the brackets

But the bands play on

Til the nets are gone

It's do or die

Til the champions cry

Yet we're allowed

To slip the crowd

Having made our bones

We can stand alone

For in this moment

and for this while

We have our own concept

We have our own style

We cheer for our teams

We cheer for each other

We console our losses

Like sister and brother

It is our passion

It is our call

It is our connection

This Basketball

The Journey Starts

The journey starts

with a hungry heart

fed by the archetypical dream

of glory not for the chosen

but for the choosers

There Is No Shame

There is no shame

No one to blame

But it's just not the same

without skin in the game

Feeling it Today

We are all of us Good to Great
Even if we Also Ran
We are pure of heart
Noble in our endeavors
Generous in our appreciations
Soaring in our spirituality
and vulnerable in our need for others
to co-create our litanies of triumph
over the enemies of hope
as we forge forgiveness
from the inside out

Home Sweet Home

Prologue

My father came out West when he was a very young man. A for-real cowboy! He returned to the Midwest to take care of his mother. I don't know how things went with the two of them, but my mother told me dad always thought he would return to the West of his youth. I came here (Phoenix) with my partner Bernice who left us in 2011. I'm thinking maybe she'll come back and get me when it's time. So I'm staying put.

Home Sweet Home

The rising sun brings hope
the setting sun brings serenity
the middle sun brings blinding despair

Desert Days, Bereft of Atmosphere

Desert days, bereft of atmosphere
stand stark naked in their azure sameness
as empty as a loveless heart
content to be introduced
by the cooing of a mourning dove

Metal wind chimes clanging quartos
at the behest of a ghostly wind
howling through the corridors
of my salmon colored condo complex
as a cloudless dusk diffuses
the glare of an angry sun

Comes the night, sacred with delight
Featuring the cosmic trickster,
Coyote, Huehuecoyotl
Cousin to Kokopelli
A mystery for the human ear
to discern amongst the yips and barks
of our neighboring bands of canid kinfolk
the lusty rebel songs and deeds
of their immortal ancestors

I Remember Winter

She felt like a live branch on a dead tree
Her snowy camouflage stripped by the sun
Inviting passers-by to snap her off
and transform her into switches
or swords

or missiles

or kindling
Ignorant of her need to save her sap
for the birthing of another tree

This Ain't My First Rodeo

Prologue

They say getting old 'ain't for sissies'. That's a bit sexist for my taste, but there is a fat kernel of truth to it. Every year brings more limitations and oddball maladies and I'm not talking about the stuff that kills you. Me, I've had a couple of strokes and a plethora of skin and eye abnormalities. But I'm blessed to still be running, competitively even. Whenever anybody asks me or my running buddy, Dave why we still run, we always say the same thing, "We suck at golf." Now if I could get my golfing friends to admit to the reverse truth of that, I could die a happy man.

My Body Remains of Two Different Minds

My body remains of two different minds

Adheres to opposing agendas

Runs in divergent directions

On any given day

I might welcome decay

Delight in deterioration

Campaign for final cessation

Or choose to kick the old sod

who's stolen his bod

all the way to the fitness center

and bid him with fervor to enter

Both dead faithful to different ends

To let it all go or make amends

opposing poles of a pine tarred rope

leaving taut between them my vagrant hopes

My Taxes Are Done

My taxes are doneI
In some sense I've won

Escaped by the skin of my teeth

The fair was quite high

for the year that's gone bye

But my soul I did not bequeath

The money I've spent

had a heavenly bent

though good times were devilishly brief

Time Bomb

Testy old ticker

missing more beats than it catches

Head too light for pounding

Restless legs in opposition

Feet finding ways to fail me

Body bound for extra pounds

Heart returned to sender

Save the Last Dance For Me

We mortals are confident recorders

of beginnings great and small

But endings carom past us

like peas in a cosmic shell game

or go slip-sliding away

like discontented lovers

Each Epic of our existence

divine in its diversity-

vast as a civilization

confined as an era

narrow as a bloodline

personal as a language

clinging as a way of life-

Defines its passing without our leave

And yet sometimes we do catch the scent

of the divine but dying organism

in time to mourn its passing

Forgive my audacity for claiming such but...

After a lifetime of pushing words around-

to explain my plight

justify my existence

or advance my ambitions-

I am now reduced to pallbearer

My fellow scribes will hang around

maybe a generation or two

but I have zero doubt

the Reign of the Written Word

will die on my watch

Goofin'

Prologue

I meant to ask a kid what the new term for goofin' was but I forgot.

Don't Want to Seem Foo-foo

Don't want to seem foo-foo

or gush a mush of goo

but as to moi and vous

the wisdom I now pursue

Is what should I wish for you

Suppose You Were a Black Hole

Every single act that can be countable

presupposes the probability

of an immutable singularity

rendering moot the point

that only one possibility can possibly matter

So it is with diet

diet being what you choose to eat

So it is with hot dogs

and so it is with me

There is nothing in the fridge or pantry

that I care a fig to eat

and nothing in the food stores

and nothing in the restaurants neither

that generate a single G of gastronomical pull

Hot dogs dictate my event horizon

Nothing else will do

Hot dogs plumped and drippy

from my toaster oven

Goofin'

Sometimes three, sometimes two
Lapping over white bread
Laced with yellow mustard
Washed down with a citrus drink
when I have it and when I don't,
a diet coke will do

Hot dogs for breakfast, lunch and dinner
though perhaps with dinner I'll have chips,
the kind you find in convenience stores
for folks jut 'in it' for the salt and crunch

So coaches, friends and dieticians
save your collective breaths
What you eat is what sustains you

So I'm eating hot dogs for awhile
Eating hot dogs for that extra mile
Self assured that any other sack of taste
would simply be a cosmic waste

But Does He Play Well With Others?

Prologue

I guess you could say this is my dark side. This section could be much larger, but I threw out all the hate poems I could find. In my defense I have been focusing on forgiveness, asking for it, granting it. A work in progress. So ¡Viva el progreso!

I am Mired in Shards of Discord

I am mired in shards of discord

Cuts that vary in depth,

in design and in consequence

Afflicted by indifference

Unheralded in redress

Beyond the balm of purpose

The Argument

I am not the facts
not the policies
I'm neither expert nor example
I'm not the doer of deeds
be they great or small
I am instead the argument

I stand outside all creeds
I speak by doing nothing
to embroil me in the world's endeavors
to sort out who's in charge
or who is wrong or who is right
or who is godly and who is not
or even posit whatever 'godly' means

I am nothing that anybody really needs
because I have chosen not to serve
And yet I'm anybody's champion
full of time, full of space, full of understanding
I am the Argument, pure and simple

If I Could Give My Mind a Break

If I could give my mind a break
from its constant pleasing,
appeasing both my need to be okay
and my penchant for inner turmoil

I do appreciate it solving problems
or bearing messages from the Sub conscience
or contributing to my creativity

But must it be so automatic
constant within micro milleseconds
Must it flood my private imaginings
muck up my relationships
and miss the point entirely
of who I really am

How can I free the slave
and from the slave be free
Do either of us want to let go
This unholy partnership
Can I at least say thank you,
but I won't be needing you today

Where Do They Go Those Precious Thoughts

Where do they go those precious thoughts

so parcel to the dawn

You know—those little gems

that flit like fire-flies across your forebrain

before you can get them dressed up

and out into the world

Hefty thoughts to launch your day

Preambles to a new poem

Gambits to important conversation

Sparks to light a love affair

Worthy gratitudes to God

Must they be so interruptible?

So apt to scramble from my scrutiny

And why won't they return

when I have use for them?

The Dark Side of Why

I did it for you, love

I would do it again

'An it please you'

Oh, I hear the chorus in my head

The well meaning cacophony

Of do-it-for-yourself'ers

Why don't they get it

Of course trees fall in unfound forests

And feelings are held back

To fester in their own propriety

But that is not my business

You elicitors of longing

Harbingers of hope

Vamps of vulnerability

You are my business

You are why I do it

Write poetry, I mean

Love, Loss and Admiration

Prologue

Well, it has finally come to this. I have done my level best to give the impression that I am a keen observer of life and a true seeker of faith. And to that end I have attempted to present a balance of sorts. But when it comes to affairs of the heart, I have to agree with the renowned Scientist Stephen Hawking. When asked on his 70th birthday, "What do you think most about during the day", Hawking replied, 'Women. They are a complete mystery.'"

I would add only that of all the qualities they are known for in the area of love, their innate understanding of unconditional love carries the most weight and the most hope for all of us.

Promise Me Not When Love Is In the Bud

Promise me not when love is in the bud

that there can be a conjuring

with the incarnations of the seasons

and their death defying undulations

such that the raging beauty of our rose

can unleash again its atom smashing essence

But say you love me today

And say it again tomorrow

And hear it said to you

in all the days to follow

And I behold a new reality

Unrelated to rearview mirrors

or telescopic projections

A new and natural knowing

Serene in its sensitivity

Facile as our fleeting moments

Accepting of each other's truth

as patient soil accepts the rain

My Beloved Other

Trying to write

Thinking too hard

Not like the Bard

Stringing pearls without regard

Always a bee in his bonnet

Could write a play in a day

And burp up a sonnet

His brain was iambic

His rhyme was titanic

He must have been manic

The stories he told

All of them bold

Even the ones that he stold

 Leaving the rest of us rabble

to lace up our babble

with unsavory quid pro quo

So a borrowing I go

A grizzled old Romeo

to whom Juliet posits these lines

"That which we call a rose

By any other name would smell as sweet."

But methinks she misses the mark

A name is not something you give willy nilly

Be you a gent or be you a philly

And though I've given you many

There just isn't any

That refer to a part

I don't know by heart

Whew! I'm nearly through

So suffer me now to imbue

My name for the all of you

I saw it and stole it and made it my druther

I hope you like it,

My Beloved Other

Calculus

Such a lovely calculus

you and I together

Despite whatever separates

Despite whatever tethers

We have traveled over time

to find us teetering on a metaphor-

perhaps the ultimate sublime

of what could be our evermore

Do we fly up beyond the endless sea

or do we fall into the deep abyss

Are we only what was meant or not to be

or are we shapers of a future bliss

Not a Love Poem Per Se

Not a love poem per se
for who's to say

What is or is not your essence

Does or does not define you

Will or will not woo you

Inspire you

Reveal you

Regale you

Exalt you

Know you

Free you

Certainly not me.

I just work here.

Today I am passing out tools.

Testing the waters

Collecting the stuff of us

From way back then to now

Dreaming of a great mosaic

A full color membrane of truth and light

The last occlusion between you

and the waking glory of the universe

When You Tire of Tilting Windmills

When you tire of tilting windmills

When the dawn no longer calls you forth

to gird your loins and rise unto the glory of your cause

You might have leave to look beyond your withered
bosom

and gaze instead into the caverns of your heart

A heart no longer brimming ore with the warrior's love
of battle-

love for the impassioned faces of comrades in the fight

Might you then my Queen give summons

To all the men who loved you, held you highest in
regard

Had privilege to know the woman beneath the garbs of
power

Had hope beyond hope to become the chosen one

Summons me then as one such man, dear lady

And know my pledge of fealty, made so long ago

Has never wavered nor will it ever still

Ode to a Friend Leaving Town

I may have given up

professing the sweep of my love

in terms of the sun and the moon and the stars

And maybe 'being as close as your next breath'

metaphorically impinges on

the domain of your Creator

Yet I proclaim a presence

in your very here and now

your temporal space

and your space beyond the trace of time

For in accordance with my wishes

and allowance for my ways

I remain with no reluctance

a photon of your essence

linked through nonlocality

mapped in your eternity

Here when you're Here

There when you're There

Not when you wish it Not

Free when you wish it Free

Split by observation

Seemingly alone

Our pattern reemerges

And reemerges

And…

Ode to Your White Rose

Seldom have I seen in life

a pairing of such purpose

you and your white rose

shape to shape

promise to promise

blossom to blossom

delicate to delicate

resilient to resilient

oneness to oneness

perfection to perfection

Our Hearts Remain Connected

Our hearts remain connected

by a thin but vibrant chord of yellow light

that defies diffusion

holds fast its resolution

is not privy to confusion

gladly supports inclusion

alive to all infusions

of the tenderest of sentiments

Our light can be intersected

by brilliant bursts that swallow night

through pulsing points of feeling

touching and revealing

truth without concealing

hands providing healing

bodies ripe for reeling

from intentions for contentment

The Untethered Text

Would that I could send you

A text untethered by desire

An ode to your magnificence

A mirror to your fire

A verse that shouts your virtues

Uncluttered by my need

A line of love that circles on itself

And needs not be replied

 An image for the heart of you

Something of your own

Something you would guard as dearly

As a Queen would guard her throne

And for my author's fee

Neither borrower nor lender be

And for Spirit's sake credit not the likes of me

I Saw You Standing In the Court-yard

I saw you standing in the court-yard

before or after church

unattached, disengaged

You were very dark

your clothes

your demeanor

Then in motion

you passed by as though you didn't see me

and I followed cautious, hiding all intent

You abruptly turned and smiled at me

or gave a look of recognition

which I took to be a smile

I moved to close the space between us,

but you stopped me with a cry

Wordless, soundless

but nonetheless a cry

that framed us in our final stand

Creature to creature

Splendor to splendor

And from your splendor came this truth

'I am not here for you'

And from mine own

'I know, nor I for you'

And holding brief a final stare

We parted

Written on the Beach a Day or So After Super Bowl Sunday

Brownish off-white sand

Rambling, whooshing waves

Twinkling acres of greenish blue

Puny clouds spotting up an anemic sky

Seagulls soaring with graceful menace

Wind defeating all attempts to give light to my cigar

Nothing in the bluster of it all

No Nepenthe to push you from the forefront of my
brain

Only surfers catch my eye

Only the curve and verve of their arc

disappearing darkly below their flight paths

only to reappear in triumph, cresting and besting

for a long, delicious blink

Then their hold on me breaks off

and my gaze returns to you

But not to us, beach-walking hand in hand

Not to us in any future knowing

Only your spirit-sprightly, smiling, sad and sage

Only your face framing the story of my never-ending captivity

And so it goes with me and beaches

As Poems Go

Is it/was it/must it always seem to be

From before the always to the never ending now

The truth was never in the how

Nor in the love and exaltation

The promise posed in relationship

Fell too soon short of partnership

Leaving me to wonder what it was that so surprised us

we felt compelled to seek the Western Wall alone

Me thinks my slant reeks of self-indulgence

in dangerous degree

In no way do I assign that fault to thee

To Say My Love for You Is Timeless

To say my love for you is timeless

Is to say nothing much at all

For time is no such thing

and life is stacked upon a spool

of untold possibilities

To say may love for you lives only in the now

Then wow, that's saying something

Because 'now' is just another way to say forever

so really, need I say more

Thank You and Godspeed

About Garry Cox

Garry L. Cox lives in Phoenix, Arizona and attended both Truman University, where he obtained a Bachelor's degree in Education, and Northern Arizona University where he earned his Master's Degree in Education, Educational Leadership.

Garry is now retired but his extensive work history includes teaching English, Reading and Writing Proficiency at the Junior High, High School, Adult Education, Community College and Online Levels for both native English speakers and English as Second Language Learners.

He was also an administrator and an award winning creator of reading based Edu-Dramas for Rio Salado College Adult Education Program and also for The Detroit Board of Education.

Garry believes that writing is a precursor to thought, not the other way around, and his love for poetry started at an early age, when his natural ability to speak poetically was nurtured by his mother. For almost a decade, he wrote a short poem for his Life Partner, Bernice, every day before he left for work. After she passed in February 2011, he decided to create the blog *Run for Your Life,* in her honor and has also created a book of poetry.

As a runner, Garry is a lifer. He runs every day and still competes, while training with some of the best athletes in the world at ALTIS World. He was also a well-known, on-air personality for a youth based Cable TV Show in Highland Park, Michigan - The Song Plugger's Kids. In addition he directed and created script material as part of the City of Detroit Summer Youth Employment Program. You can read Garry's blog on his website www.garrrycox.com or connect with him on Facebook-Garry Cox and follow him on Twitter.

Roll the Credits

Current Projects

Novels: The <u>Navaho Detective</u>, <u>World Without Midnight</u>
Plays: It Ain't Necessarily So, I Never Played Hamlet, and
<u>It's All Poetry to Me: Anthology of Good Writing</u>

Visit Garry's Website garrycox.com *for current blogs Run for Your Life, Living a Dream* & new blog *Please Introduce Me to My Higher Self* due to launch in December 2016. Also see on garrycox.com the popular blog stories of *Bernice and Garry & Me and Dad.*

Lineage and Extended family

Son of Zoe and Ben Cox
Father of Amy Zoe Shonhoff (Mom Judi Sharp, Husband Michael) and Brett McKenzie Cox (Mom Eileen Delorey and her children Matt and Amy Vujnov)
Grandfather of Scarlett and Theo Shonhoff
Honorary Grandfather of Garrett Winters and Zach Perry
Life Partner Bernice B Wagner
Bernice's Family: Sandi & Jodi Hill parents of Nicole & Kelly, Ellen Perry mother of Zach and her husband Tim, Patti and Patrick Winters parents of Garrett Winters, Sister Karen Koze & husband John

Contributions of a Lifelong Learner

- BS in Education, Truman University

- Masters Degree in Education, Educational Leadership from Northern Arizona University

- Acted in and Directed Award Winning Community Theater in Iowa, Michigan and Arizona

- Teacher, Administrator, Award Winning Creator of Reading Based Edu-Dramas for Rio Salado College Adult Education Program and also for The Detroit Board of Education

- Directed and Created Script Material for Drama Workshop as part of City of Detroit Summer Youth Employment Program

- Directed National Award winning Mental Health Drama The Mind-Finders by John Kosik

- On-air Personality for a youth based Cable TV Show in Highland Park, Michigan-The Song Plugger's Kids

- Taught English Reading and Writing Proficiency on the Junior High, High School, Adult Education, Community College and Online Levels for both native English speakers and English as Second Language Learner

Acknowledgements

(1) The **Iowa Tests of Educational Development (ITED)** are a set of standardized tests given annually to high school students in many schools in the United States, covering Grades 9 to 12. The tests were created by the University of Iowa's College of Education in 1942, as part of a program to develop a series of nationally accepted standardized achievement tests. The primary goal of the ITED is to provide information to assist educators in improving teaching.[1]

(2) The **Program in Creative Writing**, more commonly known as the **Iowa Writers' Workshop**, at the University of Iowa in Iowa City, Iowa, is a much-celebrated[1] graduate-level creative writing program in the United States

Made in the USA
San Bernardino, CA
20 December 2016